W9-AWT-107

Xtreme Athletes
Danica Patrick

Xtreme Athletes

Danica Patrick

Bonnie Hinman

MORGAN REYNOLDS

PUBLISHING

Greensboro, North Carolina

Xtreme Athletes

Michael Phelps
David Beckham
Danica Patrick
Kelly Slater
Shaun White

Madison Central School
Route 20, Madison, NY 13402

XTREME ATHLETES: DANICA PATRICK

Copyright © 2009 by Bonnie Hinman

Library of Congress Cataloging-in-Publication Data

Hinman, Bonnie.
  Xtreme athletes : Danica Patrick / by Bonnie Hinman.
    p. cm.
  Includes bibliographical references and index.
  ISBN 978-1-59935-079-0
  1. Patrick, Danica, 1982---Juvenile literature. 2. Automobile racing drivers-
-United States--Biography--Juvenile literature. 3. Women automobile racing
drivers--United States--Biography--Juvenile literature. I. Title.
  GV1032.P38H56 2007
  796.72092--dc22
  [B]

                                        2007042944

Printed in the United States of America

First Edition

Thanks, Kyle, Carol, Emily, A. J., Rudy, and Ellie Wirts for introducing Aunt Bonnie to the excitement of racing

Contents

Chapter One:
Conquering the Brickyard 11

Chapter Two:
Off to England 25

Chapter Three:
Finding a Ride 43

Chapter Four:
Rookie Year 59

Chapter Five:
Slowed Down 77

Chapter Six:
A New Team 87

Timeline 96

Sources 100

Bibliography 104

Web sites 110

Index 111

Danica Patrick
(Courtesy of Michael L. Levitt/LAT Photographic)

Conquering the Brickyard

A yellow flag waved as the drivers at the Indianapolis 500 entered lap 186 out of 200. Rookie Danica Patrick had held the lead for fourteen laps, but the twenty-three-year-old still had fourteen to go and no time for a pit stop to refuel.

The crowd of 300,000 in the Indianapolis Motor Speedway grandstands jumped to its feet when the green flag finally waved and Patrick blasted out of her restart. Cars on the 500-mile-long course easily reach speeds of up to 160 miles per hour on average, and Patrick's number sixteen race car blew by her competitors, taking the lead again.

Patrick managed to hold the lead until lap 194, when a car driven by Dan Wheldon overtook her. In the

Danica racing at the 2005 Indy 500 *(Courtesy of AP Images/Darron Cumming)*

end, she finished fourth among thirty-three. Still, she made history that day, May 29, 2005: she became the first woman driver to lead laps in the eighty-nine-year history of the venerable Indy 500—one of the most prestigious competitions in car racing. Her fourth-place finish at the Indianapolis Motor Speedway earned her the honor of Rookie of the Year as well.

Danica grew up in Roscoe, Illinois, a few miles north of Rockford.
(Courtesy of the National Atlas)

Danica Sue Patrick was born on March 25, 1982, in Benoit, Wisconsin, and grew up in nearby Roscoe, Illinois. Danica's father, T. J., and her mother, Bev, had met at a snowmobile race. T. J. Patrick raced

Danica stands beside her father, T. J. Patrick. *(Courtesy of LAT Photographic)*

snowmobiles, midget cars, and motocross bikes. An oval racer in the Sno-Pro series, he was a world snowmobile racing champion in 1978. Bev was serving as mechanic, nicknamed "Captain Traction," for a friend's snowmobile the day they met. They were married soon after, and Danica was born within a year.

Danica hugs her mom, Bev, at the track. *(Courtesy of AP Images/Michael Conroy)*

A few years later, the Patricks had another daughter, Brooke. It was Brooke who led Danica to racing. Brooke's friend raced go-karts, and Brooke wanted to give karting a try, too. Danica said that when she saw her first go-kart, "I took one look and thought,

ooohhh, this looks like fun!" The Patrick parents had been thinking of buying a pontoon boat for the family, but Brooke convinced them to buy two go-karts instead.

Danica had wanted the boat but settled for the go-karts, and the family began a new life. Brooke's interest faded quickly, but Danica was hooked. "In my first race in go-karts, I was lapped within six laps by the competition," she said. "I knew I would have to concentrate, improve, and be determined. But racing is something I wanted to do once I drove that kart for the first time."

Karting

Karting is a type of open-wheel racing and many drivers have started there. Al Unser Jr., A. J. Foyt IV, and Sam Hornish Jr. all did their first racing in go-karts. Kart racing has several different classes for different ages and types of karts. Each class has certain standards that a kart must meet to be legal to race. These standards include size of motor, no suspension system, and no differential or gearing to the rear wheels. Kart racers can be as young as five, but real racing begins at age eight and continues up through adults. T. J. Patrick designed and built Danica's karts.

Danica started in the Junior Sportsman Stock class at the local karting track, Sugar River Raceway. Danica's class included all boys, age eight to twelve. She soon won her first race when she passed two drivers who had crashed.

"I had won my first race! I had never felt such exhilaration," Danica said later. "It felt awesome. I loved winning and I loved racing." Winning races quickly became commonplace for Danica, but she never tired of that thrill. "Racing was my focus and my sole desire."

Within six months Danica was breaking track records at Sugar River and other nearby tracks. As she proved herself, the travel began. The whole Patrick family spent many weekends on the road during karting season, which ran from April through October in the Midwest. They drove the family truck to racetracks in Michigan, Ohio, Indiana, and

Danica started her career by racing karts like these.

Wisconsin. T. J. Patrick was the mechanic and pit crew for Danica and her kart, while Bev Patrick kept the statistics, and Brooke was the cheerleader.

"Spending this kind of concentrated time with my family at such a young age taught me a lot of things, including patience, understanding, and sometimes the need for privacy!" Danica said. "It also taught me the importance of keeping loved ones and those you trust close, something that would come in very handy as my career began to take off."

Danica's first two years of karting were exciting and challenging. As the only girl driver, she quickly understood that this fact alone would always make her different. The boys were often intimidated by Danica's aggressive racing style and sometimes resented her. She was the first to admit that she was sometimes a bully on the track. She later described one incident with a driver named Brian. Danica had developed a rivalry with Brian, and during a race she decided to let him know that she wasn't afraid of him.

"As we approached one of the last turns of the race, he (Brian) came to the inside of me," she recalled. "The turn was a fast ninety-degree corner. He approached, and I turned and drove right into the side of him, which knocked the chain off his kart, making him unable to finish the race."

Danica's father made her apologize to Brian after the race, but Danica saw it as part of the sport, part of the rivalry, to show her competition that she wasn't afraid.

Danica's first crash didn't come until she was twelve and racing in a national event in North Carolina. She was leading the race until another driver, Sam Hornish Jr., pushed her off the track while taking a

turn. She fell to third place but was able to catch up and join the other two leading drivers. They formed a V as they approached the last turn. Danica tried to stay left to pass, but as she entered the final turn, she didn't lift her foot from the throttle, causing her to drive right over Hornish. Her kart flipped and landed on top of him.

Her parents were horrified and ran onto the track. Thankfully, neither driver was hurt. Hornish went on to race in the Indy Series, and today regularly competes against Patrick.

Meanwhile, Danica's parents had started their own business, a glass company, when their daughters were very young. They initially ran the company out of their garage with Danica's mom doing the accounting. The business was successful, which helped make Danica's karting possible, as the weekend travel to karting events was expensive. "My parents did whatever it took to see to it that I had all of the advantages in racing," Danica said.

At one point, the family also owned a Java Hut coffee shop. Danica worked there for a while, until let go by her mother.

"I wasn't fired," Danica later recalled. "She just didn't like the fact that I was coming in twenty to thirty minutes late and laughing at it. I was a pretty bad procrastinator. About the only thing I'm timely on is stuff at the race track getting to my car on time."

In 1996, at age fourteen, Danica won thirty-nine of forty-nine races, and the wins began to pile up with each successive year. That same year Danica attended the Lyn St. James driver development program. St. James was the second woman in history to race in the Indy 500, and in 1992 she was the Indianapolis 500 Rookie of the Year.

St. James founded the driver development program to provide early experience for aspiring drivers. One of the program's aims is to help young women advance and excel in the male-dominated sport.

Program participants undergo testing to identify their strengths and weaknesses. They learn about physical training, nutrition, and how to write a sponsor proposal. St. James was impressed with young Danica and introduced her to key people in the open-wheel racing world.

"Out of 200 that have gone through my program, no more than 10 set themselves apart that I've gone out of my way to help behind the scenes," St. James said. "They have to be exceptional. It's not good enough to just be good. The reality is you have to be extraordinary. I saw Danica as extraordinary."

Lyn St. James *(Courtesy of Tom G. Lynn/Time Life Pictures/Getty Images)*

During this time, Danica was a student at Hononegah High School, where she played softball, volleyball, basketball, and sang in the choir. She was also a cheerleader until she was kicked off the squad in tenth grade for missing too many practices and games. She said that while she enjoyed cheerleading, racing was her passion, so she could shrug off getting the boot from the squad.

By the time Danica reached the Seniors Series in karting, she had her eye on race cars instead of karts. "I was becoming aggressive on the track—too aggressive to keep racing karts," Danica said. "My eagerness to move into Formula cars was beginning to get the best of me. My impatience was growing to move on to bigger challenges."

In her final karting race, Danica fell behind the others because of a broken nose cone on her kart. She took a pit stop to get the cone fixed, but was lapped by another kart; and in Formula A kart racing, if you are lapped, you must leave the race. When Danica reentered the race after the pit stop, she was waved off with the black flag, instructing her to exit the race. Danica, however, ignored the flag and kept going until she saw her mother standing on a hay bale to the side waving her arms.

Danica rolled into the pits this time and just kept going, driving through the pedestrian areas to the garage. Driving through the crowds of people was strictly forbidden, and Danica knew it.

The karting association notified Danica a few weeks later that she would not be allowed to participate in the Senior Series for the next year. It was bad news, but Danica didn't care; she had other plans.

two
Off to England

In 1997, Danica attended her first Indianapolis 500 race with Lyn St. James, who introduced her to a well-known racing family, the Mecoms. John Mecom Jr., a Texas oil tycoon, had long been a racing fan and supporter. Mecom talked with Danica about racing in England; he said that racing there was an essential experience for any young driver hoping to turn pro in open-wheel car racing.

The next year, Danica returned to the Indy 500 and once again talked to the Mecoms. John Mecom III had provided financial support for race car drivers just as his father had done before him. The younger Mecom began following Danica's career after they met.

Danica and her parents decided that the next logical step for her was going to England to race, though Danica was sixteen and still a junior in high school. "If you want to be the best lawyer, you go to Harvard," Bev Patrick reasoned. "If you want to be the best driver, you go to England." So Danica dropped out of high school, and instead earned a GED.

John Mecom III provided a great part of the financial support for the move and became Danica's manager. Ford Racing also took an interest in supporting Danica's switch from karts to cars.

In England, Danica lived in Milton Keynes with friends of the Mecom family. Central England is considered the home of Formula One racing and the developmental series that leads to Formula One.

Different Types of Racing

Formula One

The cars are single-seaters with cockpits and open wheels. They are lightweight, and technologically, the most advanced of all race cars. Formula One racing is done on street courses and closed road courses all over the

A Formula One car

world. They can run the fastest laps of any race cars.

IndyCar Racing

These open-wheel cars are similar to Formula One cars but are slightly slower and heavier. Two main series in the U.S. race Indy Cars. The Indy Racing League races mainly on ovals

A Champ car *(Courtesy of AP Images/Jacques Boissinot)*

with a few road courses, while the Champ series races mainly on road courses.

Developmental Series

There are a number of open-wheel developmental series in the U.S. and Europe for drivers with less experience. The Toyota Atlantic Series and the Ford Formula Series are just two of them. The cars go slower and

A Toyota Atlantic Series car *(Courtesy of AP Images/Greg Wahl-Stephens)*

often don't have the distinctive fins of the faster cars.

Stock Car Racing

NASCAR is the most famous stock car race, but there are several different categories of stock car racing. The cars look like street cars, and the series began when drivers raced

A Stock car *(Courtesy of the Department of Defense)*

their own cars for fun. Now the cars use specialized technology and hand-built bodies and engines.

Sports Car Racing

These cars are two-seaters with covered wheels and can be highly modified production cars or purpose-built prototypes. The makers include some of the most familiar names in auto racing history, such as Ferrari, Porsche, and Maserati. Sports cars compete on closed

A sports car *(Courtesy of Andrew Hobgood)*

road circuits and usually emphasize endurance rather than pure speed. The races can last as long as twenty-four hours using several drivers to execute complex strategies.

Drag Racing

Though there are many different kinds of cars that drag race, they all start the race from a standstill, accelerate explosively, and roar

A drag-racing car *(Courtesy of AP Images/Clint Wood)*

down a straight quarter-mile or eighth-mile track. Usually two cars race against each other. The fastest class of drag-racing cars can reach speeds of more than 300 mph for a few seconds before parachutes deploy to help slow them.

Danica was one of many young aspiring race car drivers who lived in Milton Keynes. The young drivers, mostly boys, came from all over the world to learn how to race open-wheel cars. The environment was fierce and competitive, and Danica didn't fit in easily at the tracks. There were times, she said, when it was "tough on my soul. All the drivers hung together, and I was left out of the equation a lot. They wouldn't call me. It was boys being boys."

"I got really hard over there," she also recalled. "I got really cold and just hard. I had to be. I had to get tough."

Danica began racing in the Formula Vauxhall series. The cars used in Formula Vauxhall and Formula Ford racing are open-wheeled. Their designs and engines limit their top speed to approximately 140 mph. The lower speeds make them more suitable for beginners, while still providing plenty of challenge and excitement.

A Formula Ford car *(Courtesy of Dave Peacock/Alamy)*

Danica's time in England turned out to be a rocky period, and she later admitted that teenage rebellion caused many of her problems.

I grew up in a home where pleasing my parents was just as important to me as winning races. They set high expectations for their children, and we were

An aerial view of Brands Hatch racetrack in England. Danica ran on this track during the time she spent in England racing in the Formula Ford series. *(Courtesy of Simmons Aerofilms/Getty Images)*

expected to live up to those standards. I took my parents' wisdom to England with me. And I failed . . . miserably. I got to England and realized that there were no parents looking over my shoulder. I had free rein to do whatever I wanted with my time off the track. I began drinking on a more regular basis. I was desperate to fit in with the guys, so I drank more than I did back home.

There were even more challenges on the track. The competition among drivers and team owners was sometimes brutal, and racing in England was definitely a man's sport. Danica felt that she didn't receive adequate support from the engineers and mechanics; as a result, she believed she ended up with inferior equipment. She also had little contact or support from her manager, John Mecom III, other than the financial assistance he provided.

At the end of her first season Danica went home for a visit. She found herself in trouble with her parents for partying too much, and the Mecoms decided they wouldn't sponsor her for a second season. Danica begged the Mecoms to reconsider, saying that she would do anything to regain their support. They agreed, but put certain conditions in place. Danica would live with a family in what she called "virtual lockdown."

There would be no privileges, and Danica had to be home for dinner every night.

Throughout her second season, Danica drove secondary for her team, Haywood Racing. But shortly before the Formula Ford Festival, a key event with more than one hundred participants, she was bumped up to primary driver. This bump-up gave her an old chassis that had been used by Anthony Davidson who had raced for the Haywood team and was the 1999 and 2000 Winter Series Champion.

Waving the Checkered Flag

Race flags have been used in auto races since the early 1900s, and may have been used in bicycle races before then. It was the only way to tell drivers of hazards on the track before two-way radios were invented. Today, most drivers on oval courses rely on spotters and flashing lights to tell them what is happening around the corner during the race. Drivers on the longer road courses still need the flags because of the difficulty of having enough spotters to watch all the twists and turns on the raceway. Most motor sports, including the IRL and NASCAR, use the following flags:

Green
Indicates the start or restart of a race.

Yellow (Caution)
Drivers must slow down and hold their positions. A pace car will enter the course and lead the field until the caution ends. No car is allowed to pass another during a caution period. Cautions mean that there is a hazard on the track. It may be a crash, stalled car, or debris.

Red
The race is stopped. The cars either stop in line where they are or may be directed to the pit area. Red is only used when the hazard

on the track is so serious that drivers might be endangered. The hazard might be a car on fire, a multicar crash, or a crash that damages walls, fences, or the track surface.

White
The last lap of the race has begun.

Black
It is used to direct a specific driver to return to the pit area. It usually means that a driver or team has disobeyed the rules in some fashion but could indicate a mechanical failure such as a loose hood or dragging bumper.

Black and White Checkered
It indicates that the lead car has completed the race.

Indy Cars are also equipped with lights in their cockpits that flash the same information that the flags communicate. This technology combined with the flags and flashing lights makes racing much safer than in the old days in spite of the speeds that modern cars regularly attain.

Using someone else's old chassis was not ideal, but in this instance, it worked out for Danica. When the checkered flag came out at the end of the race, Danica was in second place. It was the highest-ever finish by either a woman or an American in the English event.

Danica (right) races during the 2000 Formula Ford Festival. *(Courtesy of Jeff Bloxham/LAT Photographic)*

Danica stands on the podium with Anthony Davidson (middle) and Robin Rudholm (right) after finishing in second place at the 2000 Formula Ford Festival. *(Courtesy of Jeff Bloxham/LAT Photographic)*

Her spectacular results gave Danica something to think about.

What I discovered after that race was that up to this point, I hadn't been given the opportunity to drive the right cars. Despite the second-hand vehicle, it was better than any car I had driven during my first couple of years abroad. Given the right vehicle, I was able to perform at a higher level.

With new confidence stemming from her second-place finish at the 2000 Formula Fords Festival, Danica returned to England in January 2001, for her third year and final season abroad. For the first time, other racers, officials, and fans took note of the American girl driver who had come to a stunning second-place finish the previous year.

However, Danica still believed that her equipment and support were below par. She was terribly frustrated and so was her father, who tried to mediate from back home. The Mecoms also did what they could from the states, but it wasn't enough.

The tension level grew over the course of the first five races of the season until the Mecoms advised Danica to come home and look for a better situation. This was not what Danica wanted to hear: it went against everything she believed in and had worked for. But the managers persisted and finally gave the order the night before a race. Danica was to skip the race and return to the states.

Danica had to call the owner of her team and tell him that she wasn't coming to the race. That next

morning was a bad one for Danica as she packed to travel home. The idea that she would purposely miss a race seemed unthinkable. How could she let her team down? But she obeyed her managers, and helped by her sister, Brooke, who happened to be visiting, she packed her bags, and the sisters headed for Illinois.

Danica said later,

> Racing in England was a low point in my career. . . . I was certain that from that point forward I would work only in a situation where I was teamed up with the best people in the business. My experiences in England taught me how to deal with difficult people, characteristics, and circumstances. I learned whom I could trust and whom not to trust, and in the end one of my greatest lessons was learning you need to clear the path you walk on for yourself because no one else is really interested in clearing it for you.

Danica was at a crossroads in her career, and it would take a lot of work and some time before she could move forward again.

three

Finding a Ride

When Danica Patrick returned to the states, she found herself without wheels for the first time since she was ten. It would be several months before she was behind the wheel of a race car again. Eventually she did some testing in a U.S. Auto Club midget car, which was her first oval track experience since her karting days. Formula Ford racing in England was done completely on road courses. But any kind of race car testing is expensive, and Patrick's parents' personal resources were low after ten years of financing her racing.

Patrick and her dad hit the road to attend as many races as possible. They walked through track paddocks talking to anyone who might want a young driver to

test cars. Finding a ride in a developmental series, like England's Formula Ford, seemed the next logical step for Patrick's career.

Patrick had one false start with a BMW team owned and run by Tom Milner. Former Indy Racing League (IRL) champ Bob Rahal had set up a test

Patrick talks with Bob Rahal in 2002. *(Courtesy of Phil Abbott/LAT Photographic)*

with the team for Patrick. Rahal had been watching Patrick's progress for a couple of years and made the move to get her a ride with the BMW team. Milner was impressed with Patrick and offered her a job. Patrick's joy at finally being a paid professional driver was short-lived when unexpected new Atlantic Series rules made the BMW cars ineligible to race.

Rahal helped Patrick again by getting a start for her in the 2002 Toyota Pro/Celebrity Race in Long Beach, California. The race was stock cars rather than open-wheeled, but it was a chance for Patrick to prove herself. She qualified in heats before the race.

Racing Terminology

Aerodynamics
How the air moves over, around, and under the race car.

Apron
The paved (and usually flat) portion of a racetrack that separates the racing surface from the infield. Generally, a concrete wall or steel guardrail separates the apron from the infield.

Bite

Adhesion of a tire to the track surface.

Blister

Bubbles on the surface of a tire created by overheating of the tread compound.

Camber

Degree to which right-side tires lean in toward the car (from the top of the tire) and the left-side tires lean out.

Chassis

The central body of the car, including the driver's compartment. Also referred to as the "tub."

Diaper

A blanket made from ballistic and absorbent material that surrounds part of the engine and serves as a containment device during accidents and engine malfunctions.

Downforce

Basically, the pressure of the air on a car

as it races. Downforce increases with speed.

Grip
How well the tires maintain traction through contact with the racing surface.

Handling
A race car's on-track performance, determined by factors such as tire and suspension setup, and other aerodynamic issues.

Pits
An inside area of a racetrack, parallel to the track, where a car stops for servicing.

Pole position
The position on the inside of Row 1 at the start of the race.

Qualifying
Cars must quality to participate in a race. Qualifying normally takes place one to two days before the race. Drivers take turns running one to two qualifying laps depending on the track.

Short track
Racetracks that are one mile or less in length.

Superspeedway
A racetrack of more than one mile in length.

Tight
A handling condition also known as under steer. It's when the car feels like it doesn't want to turn, but instead wants to continue straight ahead.

Definitions courtesy of the Indy Racing League.

Patrick described this race as a turning point in her professional career. "It wasn't the Indy 500, but I was in a situation where I had to perform, and if I wanted to make a name for myself in America, I knew this race would be the perfect opportunity to go out there and get noticed." She also knew that the person she most had to impress was Bobby Rahal. It had become apparent that getting a ride with Rahal Racing was

Patrick's best chance to get started in professional open-wheel racing.

Patrick didn't waste her chance. She led the race from start to finish and became the first professional female to win the annual event. After that she tested in an Indy Lights car and also in a Toyota Atlantic car. She did well and eventually received a call telling her that if she could get a letter of intent from Rahal Racing for the upcoming Atlantic Series, she had a sponsor.

Patrick was skeptical. Promises are sometimes made behind the scenes in the race world, but they're not always kept. She decided to risk disappointment and ask Bobby Rahal if he would take her on as a driver. Although he had shown considerable interest in Patrick's career, she hadn't known whether or not Rahal thought she was ready to race in the big leagues.

To Patrick's surprise, Rahal quickly said yes and signed her to a three-year contract to race for his team. Argent Mortgage and Norwalk Furniture came on board as sponsors and within a few weeks Patrick was making her debut at a race in Toronto on July 2, 2002. It had been decided that she would race a short schedule in the Barber Dodge Pro Series as a warm-up for the Toyota Atlantic Series in 2003. In her first race she qualified eleventh and finished

Patrick racing at a 2002 Barber Dodge Pro Series race in Ohio. *(Courtesy of Phillip Abbott/LAT Photographic)*

seventh, a more than respectable first outing for a new racer.

By the time the Toyota Atlantic Series got underway in 2003 Patrick had finished as high as fourth in the Barber Series and was ready to show the world what she could do with good equipment and support.

Madison Central School
Route 20, Madison, NY 13402

Bobby Rahal fully believed in Patrick's talent, and was ready to offer his support.

> Her talent was obvious. Her commitment is what really spoke to me. There are a lot of talented people in this world who don't have the mental discipline or determination that Danica has. It's why she excels and succeeds. Danica has that chip on her shoulder that all champion drivers need to make it. . . . She's not fearful or unwilling to face any challenge. She not only wants the challenge, she looks for it. That's what champions do.

Soon, it was clear that Rahal's faith in Patrick was not misplaced. The first race of the 2003 Toyota Atlantic Series was in Monterrey, Mexico. Patrick finished third and became the first woman to stand on a post-race podium in the thirty-one prior seasons of Atlantic racing.

But Patrick didn't waste any time before letting racing fans, sponsors, and drivers know how she felt about the woman race car driver fuss. "Everyone is always looking for the latest and greatest thing, but for me racing isn't about being the best female driver in the sport, but being the best driver I can possibly be," she said. "I'll know I'll have made it when the media and the other drivers simply refer to me as a driver."

Patrick celebrates after finishing third at the 2003 Toyota Atlantic Series race in Monterrey, Mexico. *(Courtesy of Martina Luzzi/LAT Photographic)*

Patrick races at a 2003 Toyota Atlantic Series event in Cleveland, Ohio. *(Courtesy of Michael Kim/LAT Photographic)*

One of the challenges for Patrick in that first season was learning how to help set up her car to get the best performance. She hadn't learned much about the inner workings of cars while in England and had to work at acquiring the needed skills. Drivers have to be able to feel their car's performance and relay that information to the engineers and mechanics. Chassis setup and

aerodynamic tuning play a huge part in any racer's success. Patrick had help from her team members and drove many laps to acquire the knowledge she needed to be competitive.

Patrick completed ten of the twelve Toyota Atlantic races in 2003 and ended up on the podium one more time when she finished second in the last race in Miami. She came in sixth in overall points.

Patrick may have wanted to only think about the next race but there were other things to learn that first year as a professional racer. Patrick's emerging popularity was fed by the attention the media gave her. One of her most well-known appearances was the photo spread that appeared in the April 2003 issue of the British men's magazine *FHM*. Patrick was photographed in scant attire alongside a '57 Chevy; the issue quickly sold out.

Patrick later said that she didn't regret appearing less than fully clothed in the magazine. She said it was fun and opened doors for her career. The magazine appearance attracted widespread attention to the sport of open-wheel racing, which had suffered a loss of fans and media attention for several years while NASCAR was positioned to become the premier racing sport in America.

Open-wheeled Indy Car racing didn't help itself when competing organizations struggled to take over the sport.

Wrangling among organizations had been going on for years. The United States Auto Club (USAC) had been the governing body for open-wheel racing since 1956 when the American Auto Association stopped sanctioning races. The USAC took over and organized the schedule and mandated the rules for cars and tracks.

In 1979 team owners' dissatisfaction with how the USAC ran things led to a split. Several of the owners formed another racing organization called Championship Auto Racing Teams (CART). The CART series gradually pulled in the top racers and venues, but the Indianapolis 500 remained a USAC sanctioned event.

Tony George, owner of the Indianapolis Speedway, led yet another revolt in 1996 when he organized another IndyCar Series. His organization would be called the Indy Racing League (IRL). George wanted the IRL to be a lower cost alternative to CART, and he wanted

Tony George *(Courtesy of AP Images/Michael Conroy)*

it to race on oval tracks. The Indy 500 was to be the showcase for the new series.

The IRL had a rocky start with few races other than the Indy 500 and mostly unknown drivers and teams. But gradually the IRL began to pull in better drivers and teams as their schedule expanded. Finally CART declared bankruptcy in 2003, and its assets were

Patrick sits in her car during the 2004 Toyota Atlantic race in Toronto, Canada. *(Courtesy of Dan Streck/LAT Photographic)*

purchased by another organization. Called Champ Car, the revived series runs more road circuits than the IRL.

All of this infighting and change didn't help the image of Indy Car racing. NASCAR was pulling much bigger crowds at its races and with the exception of

A race car driven by Josh Hunt jumps over Patrick's car during a wreck at this 2004 Toyota Atlantic race in Vancouver, Canada. *(Courtesy of Leland Hill/LAT Photographic)*

the Indy 500 was receiving the bulk of television time. Indy Car racing could use all the positive press it could find, and Patrick had begun to attract attention to herself and her sport.

The 2004 Toyota Atlantic season found Patrick driving hard and racking up points toward the championship. She earned ten top-five finishes, including three trips to the podium. She finished in the top ten in all twelve races. She won the pole position once and was the only driver to complete every lap of every race.

Patrick came back to finish three of those ten races after she had damaged her car in multicar crashes. The crashes dropped her to the rear, but she fought her way back through the cars in front of her each time. Patrick did not win a race that year, but Bobby Rahal continued to have confidence in her driving skills. It became clear that he was grooming her for a move up to the IRL series. And that would mean a shot at the Indy 500 in 2005.

four

Rookie Year

Patrick's rookie season as an IRL driver started off with more of a bang than she had hoped for. In her first race in an Indy Car, she was running in the Toyota Indy 300 on the Miami Speedway in Homestead, Florida. She had qualified respectably at ninth and was having a decent race when a multicar crash on lap 159 sent her number sixteen car into the wall.

"I know I was going underneath the crash as another car was slowly falling down the track until I clipped his wheels and—*pppfh!*—I ran straight into the wall." Patrick doesn't remember much more of the spectacular crash that sent her to the hospital. "I had

Patrick (middle) goes three-wide with Vitor Meira (left) and Scott Sharp (right) at the 2005 Toyota Indy 300. *(Courtesy of Phillip Abbott/LAT Photographic)*

a severe concussion," she said later. "To be safe, I was held for observation until later that night."

Her injuries weren't disabling, but they were painful. She spent two weeks at home in Phoenix resting and recovering from the concussion and multiple bruises. She said she sat on the sofa with ice packs all around her arms and hips.

"In driving, crashing is all in a day's work," Patrick said. "You hope it's not part of every day's work, but it's always a possibility. My trust in my skill, my experience, and most important, being unshakable in my instincts is why I can get back in my car after a crash like the one I had at Homestead."

Patrick's next couple of races went well but it was her fourth race in 2005 that started some of the buzz about her. She traveled to Japan where she qualified second for the Indy Japan 300. The track is different at both ends, but Patrick managed it well. She led laps two different times for a total of thirty-two laps. This race was her first time to lead a lap since moving up to the IRL. She finished in fourth place, getting thirty-two IRL points for the season long contest, and won $83,700 in prize money for her team, now called the Rahal Letterman Racing Team (following a significant investment from late night TV host David Letterman).

May arrived and with it came Patrick's historic performance at the Indy 500 where she placed fourth place and set new records for woman racers. The Indianapolis Motor Speedway has been hosting races since 1909. It was originally planned to be a testing track for the automobiles of the early twentieth century, with an occasional race between competing auto manufacturers.

Patrick leads at the 2005 Indy Japan 300. *(Courtesy of Michael Kim/ LAT Photographie)*

Patrick stands with David Letterman *(Courtesy of AP Images/James Ye*

The original surface for the track was cr
rock and tar; this turned out to be a disastrous
though. During the first race there in Augus'
track surface broke up, causing accidents '
several people. The surface was redone *s*
3 million bricks, and the Speedway de
"The Brickyard." Over the year *e to*
gradually replaced with asphalt '
strip of brick remains today a'

63

A race car on the brick track in Indianapolis in 1919 *(Library of Congress)*

commemorate the old days. The first five-hundred-mile race was held on May 30, 1911. Driver Ray Harroun won that race with an average speed of 74.602 mph.

Since 1911, usually only one race has been held ...h year at the Speedway—the Indy 500. Races ...ed during World War I in 1917 and 1918, and ... years during World War II (1942–1945). In ... SCAR came to the Speedway to race for the ... the Brickyard 400. More races have been ...ears since then including several events for Formula One, which necessitated the building of an infield addition to the oval to meet road course requirements for Formula One.

Every IRL driver is aware of the history that surrounds the Indy 500 and wants to get his or her face on the Borg-Warner Trophy. The famous trophy features a small sculptured likeness of each driver who has won the Indy 500.

Patrick sits behind the famous Borg-Warner Trophy prior to racing in her first Indy 500. *(Courtesy of AP Images/Michael Conroy)*

Women Indy Car Racers

Janet Guthrie is a pioneer in both Indy and NASCAR racing. In 1977, she became the first woman to race at the famous Indianapolis 500 Mile Race as well as the Daytona 500. As the first, she faced considerable opposition. Four-time Indianapolis 500 winner, Al Unser Sr., for example, spoke out against Guthrie's 1977 appearance at Indy. Nevertheless, Guthrie went on to lead a NASCAR (Nextel) Cup race, and is to date the first and only woman to win rookie honors at the Daytona 500 (1977). The second woman to race at the Indianapolis 500 was Lyn St. James. St. James, who was born Sandra Lynn Eden, became the first woman to win the Indy 500 Rookie of the Year award. She was forty-five at the time. In May 2000 Sarah Fisher became the third woman to race here. She was nineteen at the time, and this ...de her one of the youngest drivers ever to ...pete in the Indy 500. She finished thirty-...ter an accident.

Janet Guthrie —
Fastest Woman
Behind a Wheel

"Being a Woman Irrelevant
on Track"
—Janet Guthrie

Janet Guthrie
Courtesy of AP
Images/Marty
Lederhandler)

Patrick arrived in Indianapolis with the same dreams as all the other drivers. Her rookie orientation, practice, and qualifying went extremely well, building excitement that she might be the first rookie and woman to win the big race.

When she came in fourth, though Patrick was disappointed, she was the only one. Her team owners, Bobby Rahal and David Letterman, her family, her sponsors, and promoters for Indy Car racing were ecstatic. It became more apparent than ever that the arrival of Patrick as a contender in open-wheel racing was going to give the IRL a much needed shot of publicity.

Every media outlet wanted an interview with Patrick and she obliged. Her appeal wasn't limited to race fans. Women liked her hard-headed competitiveness and saw her as a good example of what women can do in a male-dominated sport. Patrick said often that she just wanted to win—woman or not.

Within days a new phenomena, soon called nicamania, arose around Patrick. The media ry went on for months, but it wasn't all positive.

Gordon, race car driver for both the IRL and R, said that Patrick had an unfair advantage e only weighed one hundred pounds. While lifference could conceivably make some minute difference, there had been no complaints about Patrick's teammate, 130-pound Vitor Meira, who was considerably smaller than many of the other drivers.

Patrick and her team headed for Texas after the exciting month in Indianapolis. The Bombardier Learjet 500k takes place at the Texas Motor Speedway north of Fort Worth. Danicamania was especially evident when journalists and cameras swarmed around the rookie. She managed to qualify third but the race itself provided numerous obstacles for Patrick to conquer. At only 1.5 miles, the track was high-banked and the cars ran tightly packed. With relatively little experience on ovals rather than road courses, Patrick struggled to remain in the lead lap, which she managed when she finished thirteenth.

"Yeah, I'm disappointed," Patrick said, "But I'm not an idiot. I know it takes time to learn things. That's why I have these three shiny yellow lines (symbolizing a first-year driver) on my car."

There was fun to be had in spite of the disappointing finish. Patrick and fellow driver Tomas Enge had auctioned off a piece of the front wing of Patrick's car that had been damaged in the Indy 500. The two had collided on lap 154 leaving Patrick's wing mangled. An eBay auction raised $42,650 for charity, and the

autographed piece of debris was presented to the winning bidder at the Bombardier race.

Even the other drivers had some fun when it became clear that all the press attention was going to Patrick. Patrick's teammates, Buddy Rice and Vitor Meira, showed up at a drivers' meeting wearing T-shirts that said, PATRICK'S TEAMMATE and PATRICK'S OTHER TEAMMATE. Dan Wheldon, 2005 Indy winner, got in on the fun when he wore a T-shirt that said, I ACTUALLY "WON" THE INDY 500.

The remainder of Patrick's rookie season was a little anti-climactic after the fuss at Indy and Fort Worth, although the media attention barely let up. She qualified in the top five for six of the remaining eleven races and won the pole three times. But the highest she finished was sixth at the PEAK Antifreeze Indy 300 on September 11. Patrick's finish at the Indy 500 may have raised expectations unrealistically high for a rookie driver. Though she didn't sweep every race, she performed well and won the points race for IRL Rookie of the Year.

Other honors came Patrick's way as well during and after her successful season. She was the first Indy Car driver to be featured on the cover of *Sports Illustrated* in twenty years and was nominated for Best Breakthrough athlete for the 2005 ESPY Awards. She

Vitor Meira wears a t-shirt that reads "DANICA'S OTHER TEAMMATE" during the height of Danicamania. *(Courtesy of Phillip Abbott/LAT Photographic)*

was the only woman to win three poles in one season and tied the IRL mark for most poles won by a rookie. She appeared twice on *The Late Show* with her team co-owner, David Letterman, and was also on *The Today Show*, *Good Morning America*, and *ESPN's SportsCenter*, just to name a few.

It would seem that the season's end would have found Patrick off for a long vacation, but she had more important duties to tackle. She was getting married in November to Paul Hospenthal. The couple met in 2001 when Patrick went to see Hospenthal for medical reasons; Hospenthal is a physical therapist, and Patrick had pulled a muscle in her hip while doing yoga. She limped around for a month until her boss,

Patrick walks with her husband, Paul Hospenthal. *(Courtesy of AP Images/Tom Strattman)*

Bobby, suggested she go see a friend of his while they were in Phoenix testing cars.

Patrick was interested from the beginning. She said later, "Paul's confidence caught my attention right away. I am attracted to people who have the same level of self-assurance that I do. We got along from the first moment he walked into the room."

The History of Yoga

Even after Danica Patrick gave herself a minor injury doing yoga (which lead to her meeting Paul Hospenthal, her husband), she continued to practice the exercise.

Yoga, originating in India as part of the Hindu religion, is a group of practices and meditation styles used to help practitioners come to understandings of spiritual and natural matters. The word "yoga" comes from the ancient Indian language Sanskrit, and translates loosely to the word "union." The practice is intended to help reach a union of body, mind, and spirit.

However, the exercise aspect of yoga practiced by Patrick and other people outside

of the Hindu religion is *asana*, another Sanskrit word referring to a rigorous practice of physical postures and poses.

Ideally, the yoga practitioner creates balance in the body through a variety of stretches and poses. Some of the movements increase flexibility, while others work different muscles, burning fat and building stamina.

There are many different types of yoga practiced for exercise. *Hatha* is a general term for a number of different types, and typically is used to denote beginning yoga classes and practices. *Vinyasa* yoga focuses on a series movements usually called "Sun Salutations," which are synchronized with the practitioners' breathing.

Ashtanga, or "power yoga," is a more fast-paced variety, demanding constant movement and a constant flow from one pose to the next. It is one the most physically rigorous varieties of yoga. On the other hand, *Iyengar* yoga is slow paced, concerned wholly with body alignment. As such, poses are held for long periods of time, positioned perfectly to avoid injury. Iyengar also uses props such as blankets and straps to further emphasize the perfection of movement.

Danica Patrick has claimed to be a fan of *Bikram* or "Hot" Yoga. Developed by Bikram Choudhury, this style of yoga is performed in a room that is typically ninety-five to one-hundred degrees, thus loosening the muscles. It also causes the body to sweat profusely, which is believed to be cleansing and promote weight loss.

Yoga has become very popular as a form of exercise throughout America. According to a study funded by *Yoga Journal* magazine, 16.5 million American adults practiced yoga in 2005, spending $2.95 billion on classes and products. In addition to Patrick, many other famous athletes practice yoga, including golfer Tiger Woods and tennis star Venus Williams.

The couple went out for dinner and stayed in touch over the next months. When Patrick was in Phoenix, they got together and their relationship grew slowly. Hospenthal proposed to Patrick on Thanksgiving 2004, which they were spending with her parents.

Hospenthal is seventeen years older than Patrick, but this didn't greatly concern Patrick's parents. "After the first time they met, my dad told me that Paul is perfect for me. Yes! Perfect." Patrick also said of Hospenthal, "He's mature, smart, settled in his life, and successful in his career."

The wedding was on November 19, 2005, in Phoenix. The ceremony was traditional, with bridesmaids and limos, good friends, and "Here Comes the Bride" playing as Patrick went down the aisle. At their reception, the couple danced to music performed by the band Cowboy Mouth.

Patrick talked later about her marriage and compared the lessons of married life to racing. "You learn to cope with the twists and turns—when to grab the wheel tighter, when to hug the line, and when to go wider. These days I don't have to worry about navigating the course alone because my husband is with me, by my side, making this journey with me. I will never be alone again—what a feeling that is."

Patrick's rookie season was over and it was on to year two. Would there be a sophomore slump or would she tear up the tracks?

five

Slowed Down

After a honeymoon on the island of Fiji in the South Pacific, Patrick and Hospenthal returned to Phoenix to settle into their new life together. There was the usual off-season testing to do, and Patrick also drove in the Rolex 24 at Daytona in January 2006. The 24-hour race was Patrick's first Le Mans style race.

Patrick also kept busy during the off-season writing her autobiography. She worked with author Laura Morton to write the story of her success as a race car driver. Patrick said later of her experience, "It was a lot of work and a good achievement."

By early March the media interest was building for the new season. Patrick gave interviews and found

Patrick (front) races at the 2006 Rolex 24 in Daytona, Florida. *(Courtesy of Greg Aleck/LAT Photographic)*

herself constantly asked when she would get her first win after such an exciting rookie year. Typically she gave answers much like the one she gave reporter Mike Harris with the Associated Press in March. "When I look back on last season, it is hard not to get excited for this year," Patrick said, "We had a great season, winning poles and leading several races. I asked myself what is the next step and logically, I know it is winning races."

"That said," Patrick continued, "Homestead will only be my eighteenth IndyCar Series start. The stat came out last season that it took on the average thirty-three starts for a driver to win their first IndyCar

Patrick is interviewed at the Homestead track prior to the 2006 Toyota Indy 300. *(Courtesy of Paul Webb/LAT Photographic)*

race. I won't make my thirty-third start until next season. All I can say is that nobody wants me to win more than I do."

The first race of the 2006 season was at Homestead, Florida, at the Miami Speedway. The Toyota Indy 300 was scheduled to start Sunday afternoon, but tragedy intervened during practice that morning.

Patrick's Rahal Letterman teammate, Paul Dana, was killed in a two-car crash at the Speedway. Dana had qualified in ninth on Saturday and was preparing for the afternoon start.

Another driver, Ed Carpenter, had spun out of control after a tire failed, hit the wall and went into a spin down the track. The caution flag immediately went up, and Dana was warned by his spotter, but for some reason he did not slow and hit the Carpenter car while traveling at approximately two-hundred miles per hour. He died at a local hospital two hours later. Carpenter was injured but survived.

Paul Dana *(Courtesy of Michael L. Levitt/LAT Photographic)*

Team owner, Bobby Rahal, pulled the rest of his team, Patrick's number sixteen, and Buddy Rice's number fifteen, from the race out of respect for Paul Dana. It was not an auspicious start to the new season.

There were other problems to plague the Rahal Letterman Team. It had used the Honda engine in 2005 with great success. Some of the other teams had used Chevrolet or Toyota engines, but in 2006 everyone would be running a Honda engine. Any edge the Honda engine had given the Rahal Letterman Team would be lost. They were also the only team still using a Panoz chassis for oval races, which would soon prove to be a problem.

Patrick's next two races in St. Petersburg, Florida, and the Indy Japan 300 in Motegi went well as she finished sixth and eighth after qualifying fourteenth for both. It wasn't the out of the gate quick start that she wanted, but it was respectable.

May is reserved for the Indy 500 in the IndyCar Series. Qualifying and practice were scheduled to begin on May 9, but Patrick hit New York City first for a short book tour to promote the release of her autobiography, *Danica: Crossing the Line.* Patrick appeared on the *Today Show, Showbiz Tonight, Fox & Friends*, and *The Early Show,* to name a few of the stops she made in less than a week.

Patrick shows her frustration after running out of fuel during a race in Michigan. *(Courtesy of Paul Webb/LAT Photographic)*

The media attention still surrounded Patrick when she wasn't qualifying or practicing, but she found it easier to manage than during her rookie year. Racing itself turned out to be more of a struggle than in 2005, though. Patrick and the other Rahal Letterman

Patrick poses with her autobiography during a book-signing event.
(Courtesy of AP Images/Jennifer Graylock)

drivers, Buddy Rice and Jeff Simmons, all had problems finding enough speed during practice.

The combination of Honda engine and Panoz chassis that had worked so well for the team in 2005 wasn't producing the speed needed to compete against the other teams. After each practice the team made small adjustments in the setups hoping to pull a bit more speed out of the cars.

Patrick ended up qualifying a respectable tenth for Indy. She raced well, but when the checkered flag fell for Sam Hornish Jr. on May 28, 2006, Patrick was well behind him in eighth place. Patrick's teammates finished further down than she did. Race commentators said that the Rahal Letterman cars had trouble getting grip on the corners. They speculated that the Panoz chassis was at least partly to blame.

Evidently the team owners agreed because before the next oval race in Texas, each driver was racing in a new Dallara chassis. It takes time to adjust to a new chassis and to fine tune the setups for each race, and Patrick's finishes over the next three races showed that. She qualified slower and finished no higher than eleventh until July 15 at Nashville Superspeedway when she finished fourth.

About the same time speculation began that Patrick might switch to NASCAR for the 2007 racing season.

Patrick's father attended a NASCAR race in Chicago in early July, fueling the speculation that Patrick might jump ship for NASCAR. T. J. Patrick said he was there to see how NASCAR teams market their merchandise, but that didn't stop the rumors.

After the disappointing midseason slump, Patrick finished fourth at Nashville and then fourth again in Milwaukee on July 23. The two finishes were her highest since the 2005 Indy 500. She credited her crew for the long hours they had spent getting the car in shape after the chassis change.

In late July, Andretti Green Racing announced that Patrick was joining their team for the 2007 IRL season. NASCAR speculation was temporarily laid to rest when Patrick said at a news conference, "NASCAR is not out for good. It's out for right now." She went on to say, "My heart and soul is in IndyCar racing."

Patrick was also asked about leaving her first team. "I've had a very good run, a very good relationship with Rahal Letterman and Bobby Rahal," she said. "He helped me when no one else stepped up. And I will be forever grateful for that. But at some point, there's just time for a change, time for something new."

The last four races of 2006 brought only mediocre results for Patrick, including one in Michigan where she ran out of fuel in part because her crew had no

computer data from her car for the whole race. That loss brought out the competitor in Patrick as she angrily kicked a barrel after the race was over.

When asked by an interviewer later if she had seen clips of her actions, she replied that she had. She explained:

> I don't regret being mad because that's me. I'm emotional. I want to do well. I stand by my action. I think in all sports you see people gloating, you see people very excited after making a touchdown, or you see people really mad after falling out of a race or losing a game. It's just what happens. It's sports. It's excitement. It's emotion. That's exactly what I had.

Patrick ended the 2006 season ninth in the points standings. It was a decent result for a driver's second year but disappointing for Patrick because she had done so well the year before.

When asked again later about her move from Rahal Letterman, Patrick said,

> I was definitely comfortable with my situation . . . I liked my engineer . . . I thought it worked well. But I needed to see a little more commitment as far as development goes. As far as doing whatever it took to go faster, I didn't really see all that . . . it was a little bit tough, but that was the main reason.

six

A New Team

In January 2007, Patrick tested during the 2007 American Le Mans Series (ALMS) "Wheels Down Winter Test" at Sebring International Raceway in Florida. It was Patrick's first chance to drive a sports prototype car, an Acura-powered Courage LC75. "The car is really good," Patrick said later. "I'm excited to get back to an engine with traction control and a lot of things I'm used to with an Indy Car. It's fun to work on that stuff."

Patrick had been able to drive her new Motorola car briefly in December during a Firestone tire test and in January during another test at Daytona, but new IRL rules kept her from doing any substantial preparation before the 2007 season got underway. The

Patrick drives a Courage LC75 at the 2007 American Le Mans Series race. *(Courtesy of Michael L. Levitt/LAT Photographic)*

driver and her new crew only had about four days to test and practice all the moves they would need to learn so they could trust each other on the track and in the pits. Pit stop times were down to about seven seconds which meant they needed to be choreographed like a dance.

The season opener at Homestead, Florida, was the third year in a row that Patrick was not able to finish. In 2005 she crashed, 2006 was when the Rahal Letterman Team didn't start because of Paul Dana's death in practice, and 2007 found Patrick crashing as well.

In the next three races Patrick rebounded and finished eighth, eleventh, and seventh. This brought her up to

May 2007, the month of Indy. Expectations were high for her, especially from the media, who hounded her with the question, "When will Patrick win?"

Patrick was asked in an interview about the pressure she must have been feeling before the 2007 Indy 500 and if it was more than in 2006. "I guess I do feel that I—I do feel more pressure this year," Patrick said. "I think it's many things that contribute to that, though. As the years go on, you get more impatient. You just want to go out there and run up front, and as a result you're going to win races."

The 2007 Indy 500 was a rain-soaked mess. It poured off and on until the race finally had to be shortened in order to finish before dark. With caution after caution the pace was slowed considerably as the drivers coped with the wet conditions. Eleven laps into a restart after a three hour delay, another line of showers moved in and the race was stopped. Patrick's teammate, Dario Franchitti, was the winner.

Patrick qualified eighth and moved as high as second during the race but finished eighth after a wet and frustrating day. But there was still celebrating since a team member had won and at one point in the race Tony Kanaan was in first, Marco Andretti in second, and Patrick was in third before Franchitti used the rain to his advantage.

Patrick gets out of her car during a rain delay at the 2007 Indy 500.
(Courtesy of AP Images/Tom Strickland)

Patrick was back in the news a week later in Milwaukee when she was running well and battling to move up from fourth position. When she went low to pass Dan Wheldon, their cars touched, and Patrick's spun out into the infield grass. The incident cost her a chance at a win or at least a podium finish. After

Patrick confronts Dan Wheldon about what she felt was his attempt to wreck her during a 2007 race in Wisconsin. *(Courtesy of Paul Webb/LAT Photographic)*

the race she confronted Wheldon to let him know that she thought it was his intention to bump her when she tried to pass. Wheldon ignored Patrick, and she gave him a little shove before walking away.

Wheldon said later that Patrick hadn't been in a position to pass him, but Patrick saw it differently.

> On the track you have a good gauge as far as what you know normally happens inside the cockpit, and what doesn't normally happen. That was a situation where I felt like it was something that shouldn't have happened for sure, that's why I was so mad.

That shove was big news at the Texas Motor Speedway on June 9 even though Wheldon and Patrick passed it off as just part of racing. They got a chance to work out their differences on the racetrack as the race got underway. Wheldon and Patrick raced side by side down the straightaway in the early laps, but Wheldon was taken out by a crash. Patrick went on to fight to a close finish with Sam Hornish Jr. and Tony Kanaan. It looked like any one of the trio could win but the checkered flag fell for Sam Hornish Jr. Patrick had a career best finish of third. The Andretti Green Team had another impressive showing with Kanaan at second, Patrick at third, and Dario Franchitti at fourth.

It was several races later and the middle of July before Patrick had another great race. She qualified seventh at the Nashville Superspeedway and finished third again. The following week in Ohio at the Honda Indy 200 Patrick captured her best starting position of the year. After qualifying second just behind Helio Castroneves, Patrick started on the front row.

Bad luck hit the Andretti Green team on the first lap. Patrick and Kanaan bumped on the fourth turn causing them both to spin out. Kanaan hit Marco Andretti causing him to flip and slide down the track on his top. He wasn't hurt, but he was out of the race.

Kanaan and Patrick managed to recover and finish. Patrick finished fifth.

It was on to the Firestone Indy 400 in Michigan where Patrick qualified ninth and managed to avoid a multiple car crash that left her in the running for a win. Bad luck struck again when a tire deflated and forced her to take an extra pit stop. She finished seventh.

August 5 found Patrick running near the front at the Meijer Indy 300 at the Kentucky Speedway when she blew a tire after leaving the pits. She finished sixteenth. Two weeks later Patrick won a place on the front row again when she qualified second in the Motorola Indy 300 at Infineon Raceway in Sonoma, California. She finished sixth, a good finish for Patrick on a road course.

With two races left in the season, Patrick and team traveled to Detroit to race in the Detroit Indy Grand Prix. Patrick qualified fairly slow and started in eleventh position on the road course, but she ran well and escaped major problems in a couple of minor accidents early in the race. Patrick was running a distant fifth on the next to the last lap of the race when her luck changed.

The race winner, Tony Kanaan, was out in front but three drivers battled fiercely behind him for second. Buddy Rice was running second when he ran out of

Patrick (left) crosses the finish line in second place at the 2007 Detroit Indy Grand Prix. *(Courtesy of Paul Webb/LAT Photographic)*

fuel. Scott Dixon was in hot pursuit and tried to get around Rice. The two collided and the fourth place driver, Dario Franchitti, got caught in the resulting pile-up. Patrick was able to steer around the crashing cars and roar on to finish second. It was a career high finish for Patrick who traded champagne sprays with Kanaan after the podium ceremonies.

The last race of the year took place at Chicago Speedway on September 9. Patrick qualified seventh and ran in the top six for most of the race. Near the end Patrick made a move to challenge the top four leaders, but a spin with six laps to go caused her to finish in eleventh place.

By the end of Patrick's third season with the IRL, Patrick hadn't won a race. The pressure would still be on for the 2008 season. In spite of disappointment at not getting the checkered flag, Patrick came in seventh in points. She had eleven top-ten finishes including two third-place finishes and a career-best second in Detroit.

Patrick was also voted the most popular Indy Car driver by fans for the third straight year. "I'm very flattered," she said of the honor. "Every person has the ability to pick their favorite driver and it can change, so it's a real honor to receive an award from the fans," Patrick said. "I hope I can keep giving the fans something to be excited about and they enjoy watching the IndyCar Series races as much as I enjoy being in them."

Danica Patrick will continue to provide thrills for her fans when she straps into her car next season. And this time maybe fans will get to see Patrick flying over the finish line for her first win.

Timeline

1982 Born on March 25, 1982, to T. J. and Bev Patrick in Roscoe, Illinois.

1992 Begins karting; finishes season ranked second of twenty drivers.

1994 Wins her first national points championship in the World Karting Association (WKA) Manufacturer's cup in the Yamaha Sportsman class.

1996 Wins thirty-nine out of forty-nine races; wins the WKA Manufacturers Cup National Points title in the Yamaha Junior and Restricted Junior class.

1997 In last full season of karting wins WKA Grand National championship, HPV class.

1998 Quits high school and moves to England at age sixteen; races in the Formula Vauxhall Winter Series.

1999 Finishes ninth in Formula Vauxhall Championship.

2000 Finishes second at the Formula Ford Festival in England, the highest-ever finish for an American.

2001 Races in England in the British Zetek Formula Ford Championship; wins the Gorsline Scholarship Award for the top upcoming road racing driver; returns to U.S. to look for an Indy Car ride.

2002 Wins the 2002 Long Beach Grand Prix Toyota Pro/Celebrity Race in the pro division; signs a multiyear contract with Rahal Racing; finishes a season-high fourth in Vancouver.

2003 Achieves a podium finish of third in her first race in Toyota Atlantic Series in Monterrey, Mexico; finishes sixth in the Toyota Atlantic Championship.

2004 Becomes first female driver to win a pole position in the Toyota Atlantic Series.

2005 Moves to the Indy Racing League (IRL); leads nineteen laps of the Indy 500 and finishes fourth — a first for a woman; named Indianapolis 500 Rookie of the Year; marries Paul Hospenthal on November 19.

2006 Autobiography, *Danica, Crossing the Line*, is released; announces change to Andretti Green Racing.

2007 Voted most popular Indy Car driver by fans for third year in a row.

Sources

CHAPTER ONE: Conquering the Brickyard

p. 15-16, "I took one look . . . " Danica Patrick with Laura Morton, *Danica—Crossing the Line* (New York: Simon & Schuster, 2006), 15.

p. 16, "In my first race . . . ," "Danica Patrick. Racecar Driver," *Current Biography*, October 2005, http://www.hwwilson.com/currentbio/cover_bios/cover_bio_10_05.htm.

p. 17, "I had won my . . . I loved racing," Patrick, *Danica—Crossing the Line,* 18.

p. 17, "Racing was my . . . " Ibid.

p. 18-19, "Spending this kind of . . . " Ibid., 16.

p. 19, "As we approached . . ." Ibid., 22.

p. 20, "My parents did . . ." Ibid., 21.

p. 20-21, "I wasn't fired . . . " Sean Gregory, "10 Questions for Danica Patrick," *Time.com*, June 5, 2005.

p. 21, "Out of 200 . . . as extraordinary, " "Danica Patrick. Racecar Driver," *Current Biography.*

p. 23, "I was becoming . . . " Patrick, *Danica—Crossing the Line*, 28.

CHAPTER TWO: Off to England

p. 26, "If you want . . . " Patrick. Racecar Driver," *Current Biography*.

p. 33, "tough on my soul . . ." Tom Weir, "Danica Plans to Deliver at Indy," *USA Today*, May 23, 2005,http://www.usatoday.com/sports/motor/irl/indy500/2005-05-23cover-patrick_x.htm.

p. 33, "I got really hard . . . " Ibid.

p. 34-35, "I grew up in a home . . . " Patrick, *Danica—Crossing the Line,* 73-74.

p. 35, "virtual lockdown," Ibid., 87.

p. 40-41, "What I discovered . . ." Ibid., 91.

p. 42, "Racing in England . . . " Ibid., 106.

CHAPTER THREE: Finding a Ride

p. 48, "It wasn't the Indy . . . " Patrick, *Danica—Crossing the Line*, 108.

p. 51, "Her talent was . . . " Ibid., Preface xi.

p. 51, "Everyone is always . . ." Jonathan Ingram and Paul Webb, *Danica Patrick; America's Hottest Racer* (St. Paul, MN: Motorbooks, 2005), 45-46.

CHAPTER FOUR: Rookie Year

p. 59-60, "I know I was . . . " Patrick, *Crossing the Line*, 32.

p. 61, "In driving, crashing . . ." Ibid., 34

p. 69, "Yeah, I'm disappointed . . . " Kelli Anderson, "Lone Star," *Sports Illustrated,* June 20, 2005, 87.

p. 73, "Paul's confidence caught . . . in his career," Patrick, *Crossing the Line*, 119.

p. 76, "After the first . . . in his career," Ibid., 125.

p. 76, "You learn to cope . . . " Ibid., 168.

CHAPTER FIVE: Slowed Down

p. 77, "It was a lot . . . " Dave Lewandowski, "Patrick on Tour to Promote Autobiography," April 28, 2006, http://www.indycar.com/news/story /php?story_id=6423.

p. 78, "When I look back . . . " Mike Harris, "Danica Patrick Center of IRL Attention Again," March 22, 2006, http://www.signonsandiego. com/sports/20060322-1129car-irl-seasonpreview. html.

p. 85, "NASCAR is not . . . " Associated Press, "Danica to Stay in IRL, but Switch to Andretti Green," July 26, 2006, http://sports.espn.go.com /rpm/news/story?seriesId=1&id=2529364.

p. 85, "I've had a very . . . " Ibid.

p. 86, "I don't regret . . . " "An Interview with Travis Gregg, Danica Patrick and Sarah Fisher," indycar.com, August 9, 2006, http:// indycar.com/news/story.php?story_id=7309.

p. 86, "I was definitely . . . " Danica Patrick, interview by Dave Despain, *Wind Tunnel*, SPEED, http://

www.paddocktalk.com/news/html/modules.php?
op=modload&name=New&file=article&sid=49257.

CHAPTER SIX: A New Team

p. 87, "The car is really . . . " "Patrick Enjoys
Acura Debut," *Listen Live Radio*, January 24,
2007,http://www.crash.net/motorsport/alms/
news/1424100/patrick_enjoys_acura_debut.html.

p. 89, "I guess I do . . . " "91st Indy 500 Transcript:
Danica Patrick," May 9, 2007, http://www.indy500.
com/news/story.php?story_id=8797.

p. 91, "On the track . . . " Nancy Armour,
"Danica Showing She Can Keep Up With the
Boys," June 9, 2007, http://www.msnbc.
msn.com/id/19142480.

p. 95, "I'm very flattered . . . " "Danica Patrick
Most Popular IndyCar Driver for theThird
Straight Year," news release, September 13, 2007,
http:canadianpress.google.com/article/
ALeqM5jS9WOmrao6cg-LYvwLjoU3P9wt-w.

Bibliography

Anderson, Kelli. "Decent Exposure: Forget Racing. Indy Turned Danica Into a OneName Celebrity, a Hot Pinup and the Object of Marketers' Affections." *Sports Illustrated,* June 6, 2005. http://infoweb.newsbank.com/iwsearch/we/ InfoWeb?p_action=doc&p_docid=10A739D8.

————"Lone Star: There Were 21 Other Drivers at Texas, But Danica Patrick Owned the Spotlight (Even After 12 Finished Ahead of Her)." *Sports Illustrated*, June 20, 2005. http://infoweb.newsbank.com/iwsearch/ we/InfoWeb?p_action=doc&p_docid=10AC089C.

————."Auto Focus: For a 23-year-old Rookie to Appreciate Her Historic Accomplishment at the Indy 500, She First Had to Make It to the Finish Line." *Sports Illustrated,* December 12, 2005. http://infoweb.newsbank.com/iwsearch/we/ InfoWeb?p_action=doc&p_docid=10E591973.

Anderson, Lars. "Motor Sports: Racing's Queen." *Sports Illustrated,* May 22, 2006.

http://infoweb.newsbank.com/iw search/we/
InfoWeb?p_action+doc&p_docid=111A8727.

Armour, Nancy. "Danica Showing She Can Keep
Up With the Boys." *Msnbc.com,* June 9, 2007.
http://www.msnbc.msn.com/id/19142480/.

Associated Press. "Danica to Stay In IRL, but switch
to Andretti Green." *ESPN Indy Car,* July 26, 2006.
http://sports.espn.go.com/rpm/news/story?seriesId=
1&id=2529364.

Canadian Press. "Danica Patrick Most Popular
IndyCar Driver For the Third Straight Year."
news release, September 13, 2007, http://canadianpress.
google.com/article/ALeqM5jS9WOmrao6
cg-LYvwLjoU3P9wt-w.

Gregory, Sean. "10 Questions for Danica Patrick."
Time.com, June 5, 2005.

Harris, Mike. "Danica Patrick Center of IRL
Attention." *signonsandiego.com,* March 22, 2006.
http://www.signonsandiego.com/sports/20060322-
1129-car-irl-seasonpreview.html.

————. "Going Green: Addition of Danica Could
Make Andretti Green the Team to Beat."
Daily Southtown, March 23, 2007. http://
www.dailysouthtown.com/sports/310239,232SPT7.

————. "Patrick Shows Style, Substance on
Track." *USA Today,* June 6, 2007. http://www.
usatoday.com/sports/motor/2007-06-3039643006
_x.htm.

Hinton, Ed. "Patrick's 2nd Indy Lacks Glitter: Finishes 8th; Crew's Strategy Questionable." *Chicago Tribune,* May 29, 2006. http://web.ebscohost.com/ehost/detail?vid=25&hid=108&sid=a3a766 ba-f5c6-43b3-aa2fb.

Indycar.com. "An Interview with Danica Patrick, Marco Andretti, P.J. Chesson, Paul Dana." *indycar.com,* March 4, 2006. http://indycar.com/news/story.php?story_id=6045.

————. "Ethanol Will Fuel the IndyCar Series." *indycar.com,* March 3, 2005. http://www.indycar.com/news/story.php?story_id=4102.

————. "An Interview with Travis Gregg, Danica Patrick and Sarah Fisher." *indycar.com,* August 9, 2006. http://www.indycar.com/news/story.php?story_id=730.

Indy-Tech Publishing Editorial Staff. *Danica Patrick.* Indianapolis, IN: Indy-Tech Publishing, 2006.

Ingram, Jonathan, and Paul Webb. *Danica Patrick: America's Hottest Racer.* St. Paul, MN: Motorbooks, 2005.

Isaacson, Melissa. "Winless, But Still Sitting Pretty: New Race Team Has Helped Patrick Inch Closer to 1st Victory." *Chicago Tribune,* September 9, 2007, http://infoweb.newsbank.com/iw search/we/InfoWeb?p_action=doc&p_docid=11B8F3605.

Kantrowitz, Barbara, Holly Peterson, and Karen

Breslau. "Leading the Way." *Newsweek,* September 26, 2006, http://infoweb.newsbank.com/iwsearch/ we/InfoWeb?p_action=doc&p_docid=114417b34.

Lewandowski, Dave. "Patrick on Tour to Promote Autobiography." *indycar.com,* April 28, 2006, http:// www.indycar.com/news/story.php?story_id=6423.

———. "Rahal Letterman Teammates Get Acclimated to New Chassis." *indycar.com,* June 9, 2006. http://www.indycar.com/news/ story.php?story_id=6829.

Margolis, Bob. "Running on Star Power." *Yahoo! Sports*, February 2, 2007. http://sports.yahoo. com/irl/news;_ylt=AhcEp0b4a5T4AMNzciO89MA5 nYcB?slg=bm-irl.

Martin, Bruce. "Patrick Open to All Offers, Including NASCAR." *Yahoo! Sports,* July 14, 2006. http://sports.yahoo.com/irl/news;_ylt=AoB1sa XpYnAcZZ0VYwkCqy7Rv7YF?sug=patri.

Martin, Mark. *NASCAR for Dummies*. New York: Wiley Publishing, Inc., 2000.

"91st Indy 500 Transcript: Danica Patrick." *indy500. com,* May 9, 2007. http://www.indy500.com/news/ story.php?story_id=8797.

Noble, Jonathan, and Mark Hughes. *Formula One Racing for Dummies*. Chichester, West Sussex, England: John Wiley & Sons, LTD, 2004.

Patrick, Danica. *Danica: Crossing the Line*.

In collaboration with Laura Morton. New York: Simon & Schuster, 2006.

Patrick, Danica. "IndyCar Driver Danica Patrick Quotes from 'Wind Tunnel' Appearance," By Dave Despain. *SPEED*, Feburary 25, 2007. http://www.paddocktalk.com/news/html/modules.php?op=modload&name=New &file=article& sid=49257.

————."Patrick Enjoys Acura Debut." *crash.net*, January 24, 2007, http://www.crash.net/news_view~t~Patrick-enjoys-Acura-debut-~id~142410.htm.

Perez, A. J. "Patrick Knows First Career Win Won't Come Easily." *USA Today,* May 25, 2006. http:www.usatodaycom/sports/motor/irl/indy500/2006-05-25-bonus-coverpatrick_x.htm.

————. "Close Call Leaves Patrick Craving Win Even More." *USA Today,* August 6, 2007. http:www.usatoday.com/sports/motor/irl/2007-08-06-autonotes_n.htm.

Phillips, David, ed. *American Motorsports.* Edison, NJ: Chartwell Books, Inc., 1997.

Record, Melvyn. *High Octane: The Fastest Auto Racing Series in the World.* Edison, NJ: Chartwell Books, 1995.

Stewart, Mark. *Auto Racing: A History of Fast Cars and Fearless Drivers.* New York: Franklin Watts, 1998.

Weintraub, Robert. "Queen For a Day." *Slate,* June 3, 2005. http://infoweb.newsbank.com/iwsearch/we/ InfoWeb?p_action=doc&p_docid=116B9D30.

Weir, Tom, "Danica Plans to Deliver at Indy." *USA Today*, May 23, 2005. http://www.usatoday. com/sports/motor/irl/indy500/2005-05-23cover -patrick_x.htm.

Web sites

http://www.danicaracing.com
Danica Patrick's personal Web site.

http://www.indyracing.com
Official Web site of the Indy Racing League.

http://www.worldkarting.com
World Karting Association's Web site.

Index

Andretti, Marco, 89, 92

Carpenter, Ed, 80
Castroneves, Helio, 92
Choudhury, Bikram, 75

Dana, Paul, 80-81, *80*, 88
Davidson, Anthony, 36,
 40,
Dixon, Scott, 94

Enge, Tomas, 69

Fisher, Sarah, 66
Foyt, A. J., IV, 16
Franchitti, Dario, 89, 92,
 94

George, Tony, 55-56, *55*
Gordon, Robby, 68

Guthrie, Janet, 66, *67*

Harroun, Ray, 64
Hornish, Sam, Jr., 16,
 19-20, 84, 92
Hospenthal, Paul (husband),
 71, *72*, 73, 75-76, 77

Kanaan, Tony, 89, 92-94

Letterman, David, 61, *63*,
 68, 71

Mecom, John, Jr., 25, 41
Mecom, John, III, 25-
 26, 35, 41
Meira, Vitor, *60*, 69-70,
 71,
Milner, Tom, 44-45
Morton, Laura, 77

Patrick, Bev (mother),
13-18, *15*, 20, 23, 26,
68, 76
Patrick, Brooke (sister),
15-18, 20, 42, 68
Patrick, Danica, *10, 12,
14, 15, 39, 40, 44, 50,
52, 53, 56, 57, 60, 62,
63, 65, 72, 78, 79,
82, 83, 88, 90, 91, 94*
Birth, 13
Birth of sister, 15
Hired by Rahal Racing,
becoming pro-driver,
45
Marriage, 71
Moves to England
for racing training,
26
Switches to Andretti
Green Racing, 85
Voted most popular
Indy Car driver for
third straight year, 95
Wins IRL Rookie of
the Year Award, 70
Writes autobiography,
77

Works,
*Danica: Crossing the
Line*, 77, 81, *83*
Patrick, T. J. (father), 13-
20, *14*, 26, 41, 43, 68,
76, 85

Rahal, Bob, 44-45, *44*,
49, 51, 58, 68, 81, 85
Rice, Buddy, 70, 81,
84, 93-94

Sharp, Scott, *60*
Simmons, Jeff, 84
St. James, Lyn, 21, *22*,
25, 66

Unser, Al, Jr., 16, 66

Wheldon, Dan, 11, 70,
90-92, *91*
Williams, Venus, 75
Woods, Tiger, 75

DATE DUE
